D0774059

HARMONY SWEET HARMONY

by

DOUGLAS DONALD

NEW PLAYWRIGHTS' NETWORK,
35 SANDRINGHAM ROAD;
MACCLESFIELD,
SK10 1QB

Lancashire County Library

30118081964797

HARMONY SWEET HARMONY

08554292

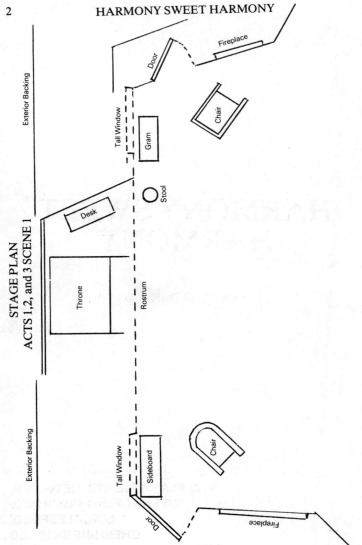

STAGE PLAN
ACTS 1, 2, and 3 SCENE 1

ISBN 0 86319 062 6

STAGE PLAN
ACT 3 SCENE 2

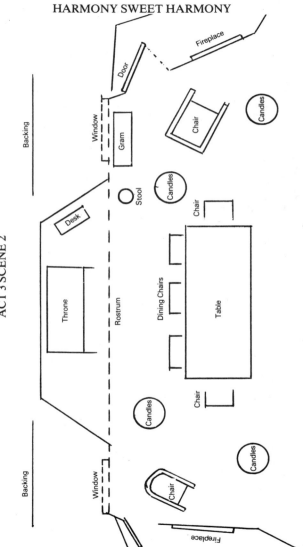

CAST IN ORDER OF APPEARANCE

LADY UNA .... A 'cellist
RANKIN .... Her butler
EMMA .... A young lady
JEFFERSON .... An eccentric old man
BORIS .... His twin brother
MISS COWPERTHWAITE .... An elderly secretary
TONI .... A young footman

ACT 1   SCENE ONE

The scene is a resplendent, but faded, drawing room. It has several unusual features. In the centre of the back wall, a large almost throne-like chair stands on a dais between two large windows. There are two doors, one left and one right, and also two fireplaces, again left and right. The furnishings on the right are heavy, ornamental, period, on the left they are modern in taste. A hanging chandelier centre and wall lights over each fireplace.

When the scene opens, LADY UNA is sitting on the throne, playing "La Cygne" on a 'Cello. She is a large stately lady of uncertain age. RANKIN, the Butler enters:

RANKIN: My Lady..

> *(She continues playing, apparently not having heard. RANKIN coughs)*
> *(She doesn't hear. He coughs again)*
> *(She does not stop playing)*

LADY UNA: You should rub your chest with goose-grease.

RANKIN: I coughed, my lady, to attract your attention.

LADY UNA: There was no need to repeat yourself, I heard you the first time. What is it?

RANKIN: I have got her, my lady.

LADY UNA: You've got her?

RANKIN: The young person, my lady. She is waiting in the hall.

LADY UNA: In that case, show her in at once.

RANKIN: Yes, my lady.

*(He goes. LADY UNA Is still playing. There is a pause and then the
door opens and EMMA, a young girl enters. She is dressed in jeans
and a sweater and carries a ruck-sack. She listens to LADY UNA
for a time and then coughs)*

LADY UNA: Good heavens, there must be an epidemic.

*(She sees EMMA and stops playing. The music continues
however).*

LADY UNA: *(Putting her 'cello aside)* My dear child, why did you
not speak?

Let me look at you.

EMMA: What's going on here?

LADY UNA: I will explain in due course. Switch off the gramophone. The first knob on the left.

*(She points to a record player. EMMA switches off and the music
stops).*

LADY UNA: I was just playing "La Cygne". That means "The
Swan". It is French.

EMMA: Really. Now will you tell me...

LADY UNA: Certainly. Take a seat.

(EMMA goes to a chair in front of the left fireplace)

LADY UNA: Not that one or there will be an incident. In this house,
it is better to avoid incidents if at all possible. That little stool will
do. Here.

*(She indicates a stool near the gramophone. EMMA takes the stool,
to the side of the throne).*

LADY UNA: That's better. Sit down. It's no use tiring yourself.

(EMMA sits)

LADY UNA: Now what was I telling you?

EMMA: Nothing, so far.

LADY UNA: I remember, the 'cello. Now, to begin with, I am not
really a 'cello player. I am a circus acrobat.

EMMA: Will you please tell me...

LADY UNA: How I managed to stay on the back rail of a chair, while
balancing a Wedgewood tea service on my nose and galloping
round the ring on an Arab charger. I was a mere seven stone, two
and a half pounds in those days. Incredible is it not? But I digress. I
can see you are anxiously awaiting the story of my 'cello playing.

EMMA: I am not in the least...

LADY UNA: Impatient? Then that is a point in your favour.
Excellent! Although I achieved considerable fame and acclaim

as an acrobat, my aspirations from childhood had always been towards a musical career. For hour after hour, day after day, I practised assiduously, sitting with my legs clasped lovingly around this noble instrument. Alas, apart from a noticeable tendency to become bowlegged, the results were nil. I had become exceedingly skilful in the action of the fingers and the manipulation of the bow; but the sound I am told, was excuriating. Unfortunately I am tone-deaf myself. Suddenly, I had a brainwave. The little black disc. I can now play the most intricate passages with all the tone, all the soul, of a Cassals. Isn't that wonderful? Well, have you nothing to say? Would you believe it? She's asleep. Child, wake up! Wake up!

EMMA: What?... Where am I?

LADY UNA: You are in my drawing room and you fell asleep while I was explaining my technique.

EMMA: Technique? What are you talking about. Who are you?

LADY UNA: There now. I wondered when you were going to ask. Such a lack of inquisitiveness is most unusual in the young.

EMMA: Well, I like that. I couldn't get a word in edgeways.

LADY UNA: Someone must keep the conversation going. That is the duty of a hostess. I remember when I was in Geneva...

EMMA: There! You're off again.

LADY UNA: Was I?

EMMA: Will you please answer my question?

LADY UNA: Certainly my child. What was it?

EMMA: I want to know who you are and why I am here.

LADY UNA: Two questions, and they deserve answers. I am Lady Una, though that is not my real name. I was christened Bella, but it was thought unsuitable so I changed it. Neither am I really a Lady. It is a courtesy title. What else was it?

EMMA: Why did your servant grab my arm and tell me you wanted me urgently?

LADY UNA: I told him to.

EMMA: Just like that. How.. I mean.. How did you know I'd be there?

LADY UNA: My crystal told me and my crystal is never wrong. It was my mother's.
(She takes a crystal ball from her bosom)
It must be kept in a warm place.
(She peers at the crystal and makes mystic signs over it)

Yes, the future is very encouraging.

EMMA: 'Cellos, circuses, crystal gazing – what is this place? A nuthouse? No. You'd better not answer that. Just tell me why I should be dragged in.

LADY UNA: Ah! Now we are getting down to business at last. That is what is known as a leading question and I cannot answer it unless my secretary is present. One never knows where leading questions may lead one.

(She flicks a desk speaker)

LADY UNA: Miss Cowperthwaite! Miss Cowperthwaite! She never answers. She's as deaf as a post. I'll go for her. I shall not be long my dear. Make yourself comfortable. You may sit on my throne if you wish. We are very democratic. But don't fiddle with the 'cello.

(She goes. EMMA looks, rather bewildered, round the room. She goes to the door on the left and is about to open it, when it opens suddenly and a little elderly man in a frock coat enters. He scarcely glances at EMMA and walks with a queer sparrow-like step to his hearthrug, where he stands with his hands behind his back)

EMMA: Oh, I beg your pardon...

JEFFERSON: Good afternoon, Sir. I'm busy. No comment.

(Pause)

EMMA: Excuse me, are you the Secretary?

JEFFERSON: Secretary! Secretary! What on earth are you talking about? Can't you tell the difference between male and female? I am Jefferson.

EMMA: All right, you're Jefferson, now...

JEFFERSON: Shut up! This is no time for explanations. I am in the midst of an important and very acute problem. Sit down! Sit down! I want to concentrate – and don't fidget.

(EMMA goes slowly to the throne and sits. There is a pause and then JEFFERSON suddenly stares across the room to opposite fireplace)

JEFFERSON: Ah! What is this?

(He quickly grabs a telescope from the mantelpiece and looks at the opposite hearth)

JEFFERSON: By Gad, he's done it again.

(He puts down the telescope and taking a tape measure from his pocket, proceeds to measure, on hands and knees, the distance from his own hearth-rug to the edge of the opposite one. He examines the measure closely)

JEFFERSON: Strange! Very strange! *(To EMMA)* Young man, will you come over here for a moment.

EMMA: Young...? O.K. *(She crosses to him)*. Well?

JEFFERSON: What is that number? My eyes aren't as good as they were.

EMMA: Hundred and sixty-four.

JEFFERSON: Are you sure?

EMMA: Quite sure. Why, what should it be?

JEFFERSON: Hundred and sixty-four.

(EMMA laughs merrily)

JEFFERSON: I see no occasion for merriment.

EMMA: You should see the look on your face.

JEFFERSON: It looks less than that to me. He's cunning you know. Very cunning. He'd gain another inch if he could. Can you think of any way in which he may be putting one over on me?

EMMA: I might if I knew what you were talking about. And who "He" is.

JEFFERSON: Boris.

EMMA: Who is Boris?

JEFFERSON: You don't know who Borris is? He! He! He! That's good. Oh! Oh! Oh! I'll let him know. That'll shake him. He thinks everyone knows who Boris is. He's a fool.

EMMA: Well, I can't say I'm surprised.

JEFFERSON: He's my twin brother.

EMMA: Oh, I see.

JEFFERSON: You don't. If you've never seen him, you can't possibly see.

EMMA: Are you identical?

JEFFERSON: *(Springing to his feet)*. How dare you? How dare you suggest such a thing? Do I look as though I look like him? I won't be insulted like this in my own half of the house.

EMMA: I'm sorry, I didn't mean to insult you.

JEFFERSON: Whether you meant to or not is entirely beside the point. Innocence is no excuse. But there is no point in offending anyone unnecessarily. One never knows when one will need all the friends one can find in this house. Your apology is accepted – with reservations of course.

EMMA: Thank you.

JEFFERSON: How would you like to be an agent?

EMMA: What sort of an agent? House? Insurance?

JEFFERSON: Secret. You could let me know if you see him doing anything suspicious.

EMMA: Your brother, Boris?

JEFFERSON: Precisely. Now you're beginning to understand. People seem to imagine that, because men are brothers, they are necessarily of the same pattern. That is complete nonsense. He's the most unreliable, double-dealing rascal you've ever met – and cunning – suspicious too. He'll never accept my word for anything, you know.

EMMA: Really?

JEFFERSON: It wouldn't be the first time he's enlarged his hearth-rug. Oh no, indeed. I caught him actually sewing on an extra half-inch one day, when he thought I was busy elsewhere. Had to appeal to Lady Una.

EMMA: Why?

JEFFERSON: Why?

EMMA: After all, if he wishes to enlarge his hearthrug, why shouldn't he?

JEFFERSON: Ignorance! My gracious heavens, what ignorance. This calls for a statement.

(He takes his stand behind a chair as though addressing an audience)

Recent incidents have made it necessary that we should once again make our position clear before the bar of public opinion. We stand, as we shall always stand, for democracy and for the three freedoms – freedom of speech, freedom of the individual, and the freedom for everyman to make as much as he can, within the law. However, there are certain unscrupulous people who have no respect for the law and it is to these we would issue a warning. Agreements are agreements and must be upheld. We are the people of peace and have always been prepared to turn the other cheek, but in the words of one greater than I, they who lived by the sword, shall perish by the sword. If necessary, we shall resist evil with force; and I would remind our enemies we are not without the sinews of strength. We shall fight them in the boudoirs, and in the boardrooms, upstairs and down. We shall never submit. Quod erat demonstrandum.

(To EMMA)

There. What do you think of that?

EMMA: It seems vaguely familiar. What advantage would it be if he did enlarge his hearthrug?

JEFFERSON: It would enlarge his sphere of influence. He is mad for power. Do you know, he won't let anyone stand on his hearthrug?

(EMMA moves slowly away)

JEFFERSON: Oh, don't go. I don't mind who uses mine. It's completely free to the whole household except him.

EMMA: Is it all right for me to stand anywhere else in the room?

JEFFERSON: Of course. There has to be some neutral territory, or people wouldn't be able to move in and out, would they?

(Enter LADY UNA, followed by MISS COWPERTHWAITE, a bespectacled Secretary, complete with piles of papers, note-book and pencil and ear trumpet)

LADY UNA: Ah, so you have met. Put the documents on the stool, Miss Cowperthwaite. And make a note of anything important.

(MISS COWPERTHWAITE crosses to the stool which she puts below dias. She fusses with papers)

LADY UNA: I trust you have been getting on well together.

JEFFERSON: I was just telling the young man...

LADY UNA: Young man? Which young man?

JEFFERSON: Why, this young man, of course.

LADY UNA: Jefferson! It isn't a young man, it is a young lady.

JEFFERSON: Is it?

(He peers very closely at EMMA)

Why, bless my soul, so it is. Well, I wouldn't have believed it. However I can see now there is something – yes – I apologise, young lady.

LADY UNA: By the way, Jefferson, is it any particular day today?

JEFFERSON: Yes, Wednesday.

LADY UNA: Is that all?

JEFFERSON: Well, we can only have one day at a time, my dear lady.

LADY UNA: I am quite aware of that. I was merely asking if it was an anniversary or something.

JEFFERSON: Every day is an anniversary.

LADY UNA: I have just observed Boris hanging out flags from his window.

JEFFERSON: He is? Good Lord. I must look into this. Excuse me, Sir – er – Madam. What the devil is he up to now? What does it signify?

(He turns at the door)

Mark my words, there is more in this than meets the eye.
(He hurries out)

LADY UNA: I sometimes wonder if Jefferson isn't at times just a trifle weak in the head. Now let me see, my dear, stand over there...
(EMMA does so)
Turn sideways, shoulders back. He should have guessed. He can't be as blind as all that. Nevertheless, I must agree that your get-up is not very lady-like.

EMMA: It is not meant to be lady-like. It is utilitarian.

LADY UNA: Utilitarian! What an ugly word that is. When you said that, you sounded exactly like Boris. Ah well, perhaps it will help you to appeal to him.

EMMA: What are you talking about? I've never even met the man.

LADY UNA: We must rectify the omission at the first possible moment. What are you doing with those documents, Miss Cowperthwaite?

MISS C: Madam?

LADY UNA: *(Shouting)* Those documents. What are you doing with them?

MISS C: I was putting them in order, Madam.

EMMA: Lady Una...

LADY UNA: She's quite deaf you know. I sometimes wonder why I keep her. Now sit down and we'll start business.

EMMA: Oh no. I am not going to sit down until I have made it perfectly clear that I am not interested in appealing to Boris, nor yet to any other man.

LADY UNA: My dear, let me explain.

EMMA: I wish you would. This afternoon, your flunkey came to me and said you wanted me urgently. I didn't know you nor could I imagine that you should know me, and I told him so. However, he was so insistent, I became intrigued. Now would you mind telling me what it's all about?

LADY UNA: *(To MISS COWPERTHWAITE)* I told you she had an inquisitive nature.

EMMA: All I have discovered so far is that you can't play the 'cello, that you are now too fat to be an acrobat, that there are eccentric elderly twins living here, but what it has to do with me and why you required me so urgently, I am as far from discovering as I was when I first came through that door.

LADY UNA: She can talk too. The gift of tongues is a great advantage, particularly to a female.

EMMA: You should know. Well, I'm not wasting any more of my time.

(She picks up her ruck-sack and makes for the door)

LADY UNA: No, don't go my dear. I realise that in the excitement of our meeting, I quite forgot to tell you why I need you. It was very remiss of me, but now if you will please sit beside me, I will waste no more of your time, but plunge immediately into a detailed account of the plot. It sounds like one of the old melodramas doesn't it Miss Cowperthwaite?

MISS C: Madam?

LADY UNA: Melodramas! Lord, preserve us.

MISS C: Melodramas? Melodramas?

(She is searching through the documents)

LADY UNA: Oh, never mind. Do sit down.

EMMA: Very well. But I warn you, if you don't soon come to the point I shall be off.

(She sits on the LADY UNA'S right on dais)

LADY UNA: Now. Has your pencil got a point to it Miss Cowperthwaite?

(MISS C. Looks up enquiringly)

LADY UNA: Pencil! Pencil! Where's your ear trumpet?

MISS C: Oh yes my...

(She puts her ear trumpet to her ear and sits with the pencil poised)

LADY UNA: At last, we can commence. The story begins many years ago, when the noble scion of this great house was a gentlemen called Aloysious Septimus Coriolanus Smith. He was the Lord Lieutenant of the County and had two sons, both born in wedlock. How many others there were has never been definitely ascertained – this being such an extensive county. His wife died young and Aloysious was a very energetic man. Energetic as he undoubtedly was. However, he, like all of us my dear child, eventually came to his last moments. It was then he made his Will – a most remarkable document, as one would expect from such a remarkable man. We should have a copy of it here, so I will ask our secretary to read from it. The Will!

(She pokes MISS C. and bellows into her ear trumpet)

The Will. She will find it eventually. It takes time, but she usually succeeds.

(MISS C. rummages among her papers and eventually finds it. She holds it aloft)

LADY UNA: Read it! Read it! Out aloud.

MISS C: Certainly, madam, certainly.

(She clears her throat and reads)

I, Aloysious Septimus Coriolanus Smith, Lord Lieutenant of this county, having to my certain knowledge, two sons born in wedlock, by name Boris and Jefferson, and they being twins, do hereby bequeth unto them, and to them alone, all my wordly possessions, monies and estate on the express understanding that such possessions, monies and estate shall be divided equally between them even unto the last farthing, the meanest bauble and the nearest square inch. I request that they shall reside in my ancestral home, Coldearth Castle, each in his own portion. This I have done because I wish to be fair to both; leaving to one no more than to the other, but, at the same time, in the firm belief that ultimately, the one with the most initiative and – er – guts will have collared the lot. Signed...

LADY UNA: All right, that is all we need to hear. Now what do you think of that for a Will?

EMMA: It seems to be a very fair one as far as it goes. Surely, these two sons could live together without all this bickering and suspicion.

LADY UNA: Ah, how pleasant to be so young and naive. No sooner had the conditions of the Will been fulfilled than each began to watch the other lest he should steal a march on him. The result has been mutual mistrust and hostility.

EMMA: The usual story.

LADY UNA: It is very foolish. You know it. I know it. They both know it themselves. But that does not make the slightest difference. As each of them is afraid of the other and both are afraid of the possible results of physical conflict, they sought for a safeguard. It so happened that the circus I was touring with was playing in this area and, having witnessed my performance and been impressed with my miraculous sense of balance, they approached me and offered me the job of acting as umpire and keeping the balance of power. Well, I realised I was getting no younger and they appeared to have an inexhaustible supply of money, so I accepted their invitation. The result is, as you see. I have so far managed to keep the peace. I live a life of ease and luxury and I am continuously letting gussets in all my dresses. Life is never completely satisfactory.

EMMA: I should say life here is completely bonkers, and I still fail to see what it has got to do with me. I'll bid you good day.
(She rises)

LADY UNA: Stop, my child! You must learn to curb your impestuosity. I have only just arrived at the part that concerns you. Please sit down again and listen.

EMMA: Oh, very well, but could you try to come to the point as quickly as possible?
(She sits on the chair on stage right)

LADY UNA: No! No! No! Not there. You don't know what you are doing.

EMMA: I'm sitting down, and this chair is much more comfortable than where I was before. I'm waiting.

LADY UNA: Oh dear, Oh dear. Well, don't say I didn't warn you...Make a note of that Miss Cowperthwaite. It was against my advice. I warned her. In triplicate... You are a very headstrong person, and I really am beginning to have serious doubts of the efficaciousness of my crystal and if I lose faith in that, what is there left to believe in?

EMMA: What is all this nonsense about your crystal?

LADY UNA: Nonsense? Nonsense did you say? My dear child, long before you were drooling your milk down your bib, my mother was famous as the Queen of the Gypsies. She and her crystal were sought after throughout the length and breadth of this land and beyond. It was the most lucrative racket on the fairground.

EMMA: You're off again.

LADY UNA: Off?

EMMA: Why can't you stick to the point? You will go on, yackity, yak, about anything but the subject in hand.

LADY UNA: Now, if you will allow me to proceed...

EMMA: Delighted.

LADY UNA: Thank you. Where was I? Where had I got to Miss Cowperthwaite?

MISS C: You had just inherited...

LADY UNA: No! No! No! That has nothing to do with it. I remember! I told you I was managing to maintain the peace, but it was becoming increasingly more difficult. Both Boris and Jefferson were getting extremely peevish with each other. At such moments it has been my practice to find some harmless distraction for them. I consulted my crystal and when I saw you, I realised what I must do. The boys, I always think of them as boys, are rather advanced in years, and it is highly improbable that either of them will have children. They are not married and neither of them takes after their father. But if they could have a ward, an adopted daughter, then this new distraction would canalise their activities into more peaceful regions.

EMMA: And you want me to be the adopted daughter of two dotty old men? No thank you.

LADY UNA: Wait, my child. Do not be so impetuous.

EMMA: Besides, I've got to go back to my job in another ten days.

LADY UNA: And you shall. These periods of peevishness do not last long and once they have passed all is well again. A week's time and the moon will be waning.

EMMA: And my holidays will have waned.

LADY UNA: You would live like a queen, or even a pop star. Dress, food, distractions, whatever you wished would be yours to command. Money is practically unlimited. You could name your own salary.

EMMA: Say that again!

LADY UNA: I said you could name your own salary.

EMMA: Oh, that puts a different complexion on the matter. Will you give me time to think it over?

LADY UNA: I am afraid that time is one thing that is in short supply. Alas, my mirror tells me so each morning.
(A trumpet can be heard off stage right, it is coming nearer)

EMMA: Good lord! What's that? Boy Scouts?

LADY UNA: I fear it is Boris and in a martial mood.
(The trumpet sounds again. The door right opens and BORIS enters. He is wearing a dark siren suit and blowing a toy trumpet. He marches in a stiff military manner round the room, and salutes LADY UNA, as he passes her. He comes to attention in front of JEFFERSON'S hearthrug and taking a pace forward, deliberately kicks at the rug. He then turns and shouts)

BORIS: I won't have it! I won't stand for it! Do you hear? I won't stand for it. This is provocation.

LADY UNA: Boris, my dear, what is all this noise about?
(To MISS C) Take it down Miss Cowperthwaite. Take it down.

BORIS: I have been insulted! Once again my most cherished

traditions have been the object of mockery. This shall not go unavenged.

LADY UNA: Oh dear. I do believe there's been another incident.

BORIS: Incident! Incident! Incident! It's aggression.

LADY UNA: Boris! Boris! Calm yourself. Nothing is accomplished in anger. You know I am here to listen to you and to arbitrate. If you have a complaint to make, then make it in a calm and dignified manner.

BORIS: Calm and dignified. Fiddlesticks!

LADY UNA: Now, now, now. Temper! You know you can trust Aunty Una. She is waiting as always, to listen, to you and to arbitrate. Come dear boy, tell aunty your troubles.

BORIS: Oh, very well. It's that sly old hypocrite, Jefferson, again. As you know, today is the anniversary of one of my greatest achievements!

LADY UNA: Is it?

BORIS: It was on this day, twelve months ago, that I succeeded in breeding Matilda, the first budgerigar to be born with four wings.

LADY UNA: Dearest Heaven. How time flies.

BORIS: To celebrate this glorious achievement, I decorated my balcony on the East wing with flags and bunting and a six-foot by four portrait of myself as the centre piece. Six feet by four! It looked very tasteful, I don't mind telling you. Can you imagine it?

LADY UNA: I am trying to.

BORIS: Thank you. I was standing admiring the effect when, and this shows the guile, the treachery within the breast, I observed a movement on the balcony connecting the East and West wings. It was Jefferson. He had crept surreptitiously along the balcony and then, taking a pea-shooter out of his pocket, he proceeded to shoot at my picture. At my picture! Naturally, I retaliated immediately with a large sized chunk of masonry, unfortunately missing him, but breaking one of the windows in the South gallery. However, it served its purpose and he beat a hasty retreat. I then examined the portrait and discovered sticking to it, several clots of chewed paper, he had used as missiles, and this proves the complete decadence of the man – chewed-up portions of the Financial Times...I demand satisfaction...this envy, this jealousy...

LADY UNA: Boris!

BORIS: Must be eliminated. I shall...do something.

LADY UNA: Boris, my dear. I have a surprise for you.

BORIS: Are you trying to wheedle me again?

LADY UNA: I think you'll like it.

BORIS: What is it?

LADY UNA: Look behind you.

(BORIS turns and for the first time, sees EMMA sitting in his chair)

BORIS: No! What is this?

EMMA: Good afternoon.

BORIS: This is his doing. He told you to sit there.

EMMA: No one told me to sit here. I chose this chair because it looked comfortable and it is…

BORIS: Get out! Get out at once! Before I throw you out.

LADY UNA: I warned her. I warned her. We've got a note of it in triplicate.

BORIS: That's my hearthrug and my chair. I allow no-one there without my permission.

EMMA: But chairs are for sitting on and I'm doing no harm.

BORIS: How do I know you're not? How do I know you're not one of his spies?

EMMA: Now listen to me. I was tired and I wanted to sit down. Naturally I chose the most comfortable seat I could find, this one. I could just as easily have sat in one of those modern atrocities over there, but I didn't I chose yours.

BORIS: You think those are atrocities do you?

EMMA: Oh, they have clean modern lines, but they're darned uncomfortable to sit on.

BORIS: Umph! He wouldn't like to hear you say that. But it's true you know. Bourgeois atrocities. You appear to be a person of discrimination. Nevertheless, I cannot break my inflexible rule. Without my express permission, no one sits there.

EMMA: But you weren't here to give it. If I'd waited until you turned up, I should have been completely exhausted.

BORIS: Are you going to vacate that chair or are you not?

EMMA: Well, of course, if you decide to turn me out, I can't stop you. You're much bigger than I am.

LADY UNA: No violence, Boris! We can't have violence.

BORIS: As you know, I am always the last to resort to brute force, but I must warn you, my patience is rapidly becoming exhausted. Good Heavens! This is subterfuge! He has planted this individual here to distract my attention while he can return to his nefarious

attack upon my decorations, the villain. To arms! To arms!
(He blows his trumpet and charges to the door where he stops and turns to EMMA)
I'll deal with you later. Rally! Rally!
(He blows his trumpet and goes)

EMMA: And you expect me to adopt him as a step-father?

LADY UNA: No, my dear child. You've got it all wrong. He is to adopt you as his niece. At least, that was my original intention, but now, I am afraid you have completely ruined my whole scheme. You really should have been more co-operative. Boris will never forgive you now. I think you had better go.

EMMA: But, I'm not at all certain that I want to go now, if there's money in it.

LADY UNA: What do you mean, child?

EMMA: I've decided that I want to stay. I'll do what you want me to do – if we can come to terms.

LADY UNA: You have offended Boris, and at a most inopportune moment too. You wouldn't listen to my advice. I told you that Boris could be difficult. I am afraid you have not the requisite tact. I am sorry because I am sure my plan was a good one, and now there is danger of the whole situation getting out of hand.

EMMA: In that case I'd better stay and help you to get it under control.

LADY UNA: Impossible. One doesn't extinguish a fire with parafin. After what just occurred the mere sight of you would send Boris beserk.

EMMA: But he wouldn't know it was me.

LADY UNA: My dear child! He's not barmy.

EMMA: That's a thought. Look, Jefferson thought I was a man, and I was standing up then. Well, I'm still wearing my jeans, but in addition to that I was sitting down when Boris saw me.

LADY UNA: That is true. You've got a point there. I noticed he ignored your legs. If he'd thought they belonged to a member of the opposite sex, he would never have taken his eyes off them. When I rode round the ring in tights, balancing the Wedgewood dinner service on my nose, the men never looked at the crockery. Yes, you are undoubtedly right. Have you a dress you can wear?

EMMA: I have a skirt in my ruck-sack, though it isn't particularly elegant.

LADY UNA: It will answer our purpose for the time being. At least you will look like a female; not even Jefferson could mistake you for a Scottish Highlander. Well that's settled then.

EMMA: Not quite.

LADY UNA: Don't tell me you've changed your mind again.

EMMA: There's just one thing – the bread.

LADY UNA: The what, child?

EMMA: The lolly – wages.

LADY UNA: Ah yes. We used to call it the "dibs". I'd completely overlooked that.

EMMA: I hadn't.

LADY UNA: When one has all the money one wants, one forgets all about it. Will two hundred pounds be all right?

EMMA: Two hundred pounds! Do you mind if I sit down again.

LADY UNA: Well shall I say two hundred and fifty pounds.

EMMA: Please.

LADY UNA: Is that satisfactory?

EMMA: When do I start?

LADY UNA: We had better begin to make our plans at once.

EMMA: This is going to be fun.

LADY UNA: There is nothing in the least humorous about it. You don't appear to realise that we are on the verge of a crisis.

EMMA: Do you realise I've got to be back at work in ten days' time?

LADY UNA: If we have not accomplished our aim by then, we never shall. To action! Oh I feel invigorated. Tra-la-la-la.
(She begins to hum and waltz around the room)
In the old days, when I felt on top of the world, do you know what I used to do?

EMMA: What?

LADY UNA: Stand on my head.
(She bends down on the floor and kicks her legs ineffectively.
Perhaps I'd better not. One should never attempt to repeat yesterday's triumphs. It only results in the realisation that one is a day older... Miss Cowperthwaite! Miss Cowperthwaite! Good heavens, she's asleep now.
(She puts the ear trumpet to MISS C'S ear and shouts)
Miss Cowperthwaite!
(MISS COWPERTHWAITE screams, jumps and knocks over the stool with all the papers).

MISS C: Oh dear! Oh dear! Oh my heart!

LADY UNA: There now! Just when you want her to take down

details, she throws the documents all over the place.

MISS C: I'm sorry madam. I'll put them all in order again.

LADY UNA: Just pick them up. It doesn't matter about the order; they'll make just as much sense and while you're doing that I'll go and get the money.

EMMA: Oh, it doesn't matter now, really it doesn't.

LADY UNA: Always get your money before you do your act if you can, my dear. There may not be any in the till when you've finished.

(She goes to the door)

Have you had anything to eat?

EMMA: Not since lunch.

LADY UNA: There's time for a snack. Would you like caviare, a porterhouse steak or roast chicken or lobster thermidor?

EMMA: Oh no, a boiled egg...

LADY UNA: You'll never last the course. I'll send them all and then you can make up your mind. Above all, fortify yourself for the struggle. *(Exit)*

(MISS C is on hands and knees collecting the papers)

EMMA: I'll give you a hand.

(She kneels and helps)

MISS C: Thank you.

(Pause)

MISS C: She's quite right you know. They'll make just as much sense whatever order they're in.

EMMA: Why do you take these notes.

MISS C: I haven't the faintest idea. I've been doing it for ten years now, but I've never known what for. Still it's something to do.

EMMA: There, that's the lot.

(She hands the papers to MISS C)

MISS C: Thank you, Oh thank you. That was most kind. Do you mind if I talk to you?

EMMA: Not at all.

MISS C: It is very seldom I get the opportunity to talk to anyone.

(She turns to the papers on stool)

EMMA: Just a moment.

MISS C: Yes Miss?

(She turns)

EMMA: You heard what I said.

MISS C: Oh yes. Yes I heard you quite distinctly.

EMMA: But I thought you were deaf.

MISS C: Well, not really. It's her Ladyship. She shouts so much it deafens me and then I get nervous and that makes me worse, until I can't hear a word. But I can hear you very well, very well indeed. Oh, it is a pleasant change to hold a conversation with someone. You see, there is only her Ladyship, and I find I can never hold a conversation with her. She's either too busy to talk, or else she just keeps on talking and I never get the opportunity.

EMMA: I can understand that. How you've stuck it for ten years beats me.

MISS C: Oh, she's very kind to me. Very kind indeed. I never want for anything and the work isn't very exacting. It's just that...

EMMA: Yes.

MISS C: One gets so out of touch. Many years ago when I was much younger and something of a gay spark, well gayer than I am now, I used to go out frequently. Ah, yes, I remember on special occasions, my sister and I used to go to dances at the Assembly Hall. Respectable dances of course. Ah dear. How well I remember when I first learned to dance the Charleston. It was so thrilling. Often my thoughts go back to those days. Particularly on Friday nights. All the big dances are on Friday nights. The music – the gay companions – the beautiful dresses. Ah me... Do they still dance the Charleston at the Assembly Hall.

EMMA: *(After a pause)* Yes.

MISS C: I'm so glad. It was a gay... a thrilling dance.

EMMA: Do you never go to dances now?

MISS C: Oh no! Oh dear no! I don't think... you see I've never been anywhere for years.

EMMA: Well, there isn't much future in living like that.

MISS C: Oh, I don't mind. The future doesn't really matter if you've got a past... I mean pleasant memories.

EMMA: How you can put up with living with these queer people is beyond me.

MISS C: Oh, they're not queer really. Not really, when you get to understand them. It's just that their way of behaving is different.

EMMA: You don't intend to stay in this job indefinitely do you?

MISS C: Oh, I hope so, indeed I hope so. If I lost this position, I don't know what I should do. Really I don't. Oh dear!

EMMA: What's the matter?

MISS C: You frighten me.

EMMA: I'm sorry. I didn't mean to. Why are you afraid?

MISS C: I wouldn't know what to do or where to go. I have no relations, no companions and really very little of what you might call life, but at least I have security. Oh dear. You must excuse me. I...

(She gathers her papers and runs out)

EMMA: The poor, timid soul.

(She goes to her ruck-sack an takes out a skirt which she puts on over her jeans. As she is taking off her jeans, RANKIN enters and crosses towards door right. He is wearing a steel helmet and a gas mask case over his shoulder. He is carrying a pigeon.)

RANKIN: I beg your pardon, Miss.

EMMA: Granted. Here what's going on? Civil Defence?

RANKIN: No Miss, I am proceeding to the East wing.

EMMA: But why the tin hat?

RANKIN: I understand Master Boris is conducting certain scientific experiments this afternoon.

EMMA: What sort of experiments?

RANKIN: I am afraid they are top secret Miss, but I understand there could be miscalculations.

EMMA: Is that a pigeon you've got there?

RANKIN: It is a pigeon Miss.

EMMA: Is that part of the experiment?

RANKIN: No Miss. I am returning it to Master Boris. It brought a message to say he wanted me urgently.

EMMA: But haven't you a house 'phone?

RANKIN: Master Boris refuses to use it since he discovered that his brother could listen to his conversations.

(He goes to door right and then turns)

Any other questions, Miss?

EMMA: As a matter of fact there is. Do you get paid regularly here?

RANKIN: In monetary matters, I am afraid my lady is inclined to be rather forgetful.

EMMA: A bit dicey eh?

RANKIN: Decidedly. If I might make a suggestion, Miss, I should beat it out of here as fast as you can flippin' well move.

(He goes)

EMMA: Right.

(She stuffs her jeans into the ruck-sack and makes for the mirror. As she gets to the mirror, TONI enters. TONI enters stage left carrying a

small collapsible table which he erects in the centre. He is young and dressed in workaday clothes. EMMA sees him through the mirror, turns to inspect him better and then turns back to the mirror.

TONI: Excuse me, Miss.

EMMA: Hello!

TONI: Good afternoon, Miss.

(He doesn't look at her but goes to side-board and brings a cloth which he spreads, and then various condiments, cutlery etc. which he lays on the table. All this movement takes place during the following conversation with EMMA following him about)

EMMA: I haven't seen you before.

TONI: No Miss. Are you the young lady?

EMMA: I expect so. I haven't seen any others.

TONI: My instructions are to prepare a meal for a young lady.

EMMA: That's me. You're the first young man I've seen, too.

TONI: I expect so, Miss.

EMMA: Are you a servant – a footman?

TONI: A kind of footman, Miss.

EMMA: There's no need for you to hurry. I'm not dying of starvation.

TONI: I'm glad to hear it, Miss.

EMMA: Do I look as though I am dying of starvation!

TONI: I haven't taken particular notice, Miss.

EMMA: No, you haven't have you?

(Pause)

Can't you stop for a moment, I want to talk to you.

TONI: I'm sorry, Miss. I have my work to do.

EMMA: You are coming back, I hope.

TONI: I am going for your food, Miss. I shall return immediately.

(He goes out, left. She begins to sing and dances across to a mirror to tidy her hair and apply lipstick. RANKIN enters right)

EMMA: Hello! Any good explosions lately?

RANKIN: It was tea-break Miss.

EMMA: Just a minute. Are there any female servants in this house?

RANKIN: There are two. A maid and a cook.

EMMA: Young, middle-aged, old?

RANKIN: Drawing a bow at a venture Miss. I should say they are both a charitable sixty.

EMMA: Good! And sex?

RANKIN: Barely discernable, Miss.

EMMA: Great.

RANKIN: May I ask why you are interested?

EMMA: Just wondering what the strength of the opposition was.

RANKIN: Opposition?

EMMA: It's all right. There isn't any.

RANKIN: Am I to tell Lady Una you are leaving us?

EMMA: I've changed my mind. The situation has become much more attractive.

RANKIN: I can't imagine why, Miss, but if you will permit me to say so, it's your funeral.

(He goes. EMMA tidies herself and sits on the throne)

CURTAIN

END OF ACT ONE

ACT 2   SCENE ONE

(The action is continuous. TONI returns pushing a dumb waiter on which are all kinds of food)

EMMA: Good Lord! What's all that?

TONI: Food, Miss.

EMMA: Do you mean to say all that is for me?

RANKIN: Yes, Miss.

EMMA: It's overfacing. Oh, for Pete's sake stand still. Don't you know it's very rude to keep moving about when a lady is talking to you.

TONI: No, Miss. I'm sorry, Miss.

EMMA: Does it hurt you to look at me?

TONI: No, Miss.

EMMA: Yes, Miss. No, Miss. Don't you want to talk to me? I'm not as ugly as all that, am I?

TONI: You're not at all ugly Miss.

EMMA: Thank you. What's your name?

TONI: Everyone calls me Toni.

EMMA: My name is Emma. You can call me that if you like.

TONI: Thank you, Miss.

EMMA: Emma.

TONI: Miss Emma.

(He starts work again)

EMMA: Don't you ever stop working?

TONI: I have a lot to do, Miss.

EMMA: When is your day off?

TONI: I don't have a day off, Miss.

EMMA: You mean you work seven days a week?

TONI: Yes, Miss.

EMMA: All the year round?

TONI: Yes Miss.

EMMA: But they can't do that. How long has this been going on?

TONI: I've always worked here. I was born in the Castle, Miss.

EMMA: But... Oh, I'll see the old lady about this.

TONI: Oh no. Please. I don't mind. I don't want a day off. I wouldn't
know what to do if I wasn't working.

EMMA: What about your wife? She must never see you.

TONI: I'm not married, Miss.

EMMA: Your girl friend then?

TONI: I haven't got a girl friend either.

EMMA: Really! Don't you wish you had one?

TONI: I've never thought about i?

EMMA: You haven't? Don't you have any ... feelings?

TONI: What kind of feelings, Miss?

EMMA: 'Struth! About the opposite sex. There are two sexes you
know. Have you never dated a girl?

TONI: The only females I know are the maid and the cook.

EMMA: I see what you mean. D'you mean to say you've never met
any girls of your own age?

TONI: No, Miss.

EMMA: *(With a whistle)* Virgin soil. Do I looked like either the maid
or the cook? Well... do I-
(He looks but doesn't answer).
Well, say something. Surely it doesn't take you so long to decide. I
can't say I feel very flattered.

TONI: Oh!

EMMA: Oh, what?

TONI: You shouldn't have asked me to do that.

EMMA: To do what?

TONI: To look at you.

EMMA: Why?

TONI: It was very disturbing.

EMMA: Good. I was beginning to think either I was slipping or you
weren't normal.

TONI: But I don't want to be disturbed.

EMMA: You'll get used to it and then you'll like it. You'll see. I'll tell you something. You'll never be the same again. You may think you're going to put me out of your mind, but you won't be able to. And if you didn't realise before that your life lacked something, you will from now on. Look into my eyes... deep into my eyes... come on... what do you see? What do you see?
(She has come close to him and for a moment he looks into her eyes and then breaks away).

TONI: You food's getting cold.

EMMA: Damn, damn, damn, damn, damn.

TONI: There's caviare, fresh trout done in butter, a cold chicken salad, a nice piece of steak, if it hasn't gone cold with all your talking, lemon meringue, pineapple tart, clotted cream, ice cream...

EMMA: Stop it! Stop it! Stop it! I don't want any of your filthy food. Take it away! Take it away before I'm sick! ...I hate you. Hate you!
(She is sobbing with rage and beats him with her fists. She stops and says very quietly)
I'm sorry. I'm not hungry.
(LADY UNA sails into the room)

LADY UNA: Ah, my dear child. I regret I have been so long. I hope you haven't been bored.
(She sees TONI)
I don't suppose you have... Take the food away, young man, and the chair and the table, and as quickly as possible...
(To EMMA)
I trust you had enough.
(TONI wheels the dumb waiter out)
I had to go and remonstrate with Jefferson. Although I couldn't really blame him. I find it impossible to conceive of anything more revolting than a six-foot by four portrait of Boris. Ah, I see you have put on your skirt. Now let me look at you my child.
(EMMA doesn't wish her to see she has been crying and stands with her back to her)
Come, come, come. Turn round.
(She turns EMMA to face her)
Why, the child's been crying.

EMMA: *(Shrugging her away)* Oh, no I haven't.

LADY UNA: It's no use denying it. Do you think I'd have given you a second thought with eyes like that? Look at them, like two peep holes in a red blanket. What's gone wrong now? Surely it wasn't that brawny lout. If he can bring tears to a young girl's eyes in the fifteen minutes I've been out of the room he's more dangerous than I thought he was. Come now, child, I never cried as much as this for a man, even after I'd lived with him for two years.

(EMMA turns round)

EMMA: Well?

LADY UNA: That's better. But we can't have this sort of thing. It's only to be expected that you'd be drawn to a nice hunk of beef like young Toni, but you're here to be the ward of two old men, not the bride of the scullery boy. Work before pleasure you know.

EMMA: Pleasure! That boy's darned hard work.

LADY UNA: All men are sooner or later. Where there's a man, no woman need be out of work. But to business! To business! Let me look at you.

(TONI enters and collects the cutlery and cloth which he takes back to the sideboard during the next conversation. LADY UNA examines EMMA)

No. No. It won't do. That skirt may indicate that you are a female, but it's femininity is extremely limited. It's a mass of creases.

EMMA: So would you be if you had been screwed up in a ruck-sack.

LADY UNA: The point is I would never allow that to happen to me, if it were possible, and what is it made of? Potato bags?

EMMA: Certainly not. It is quite an expensive tweed.

LADY UNA: Expense has nothing whatever to do with it. Tweed! Don't you know that the first essential for a young girl is to be feminine? Youth should wear silks, organzas, taffetas. She should rustle sibilently when she moves and be smooth to the touch. You look like something to be thrown across a sweating horse.

(At this TONI giggles and EMMA who has been very conscious of his presence, tosses her head)

Still, we must make the best of what we've got for the time being. I've no doubt we'll be able to fit you out in something prettier. That skirt is far too long. Your legs, I seem to remember are quite pretty.

(She lifts EMMA'S skirt)

Yes, we mustn't hide those.

(TONI has stopped to look and EMMA, seeing him, pulls down her skirt)

Attend to your work, young man. You can't do it efficiently with high blood pressure. Your hair is passable, what there if of it. I like to see more curls, but yours is short and we can't curl what isn't there. Your figure is quite excellent.
(She looks to see if TONI is working, but fortunately he is just a shade quicker than she is)
Ah, youth, youth. How long ago it seems. Yes, I am envious. Age is a dubious achievement and I have served sixty years' apprenticeship. But youth, ah youth, is an act of God.
(She turns to TONI)
Have you finished yet? It's taking you a long time.

TONI: I have had much to detain me, Madam, but I've finished now.
(He folds the table and takes it out. At the door he manages to catch EMMA'S eye. She puts out her tongue. He goes)

EMMA: Now listen to me, Lady Una. I know I've agreed to fall in with your plans, but not until you keep your side of the bargain. You said you were going for my two hundred and fifty pounds. I haven't seen it yet.

LADY UNA: My dear child! In the rush of events and the excitement of the moment, I had completely overlooked it. But you shall have it, never fear.

EMMA: When?

LADY UNA: We'll make it three hundred pounds shall we? Now time is flying and we have so much to do. Come with me, I will show you your room. You'll want to wash before you meet the boys, and if you use make-up, use it discreetly. I would prefer your cheeks to shine like well rubbed apples.
(They go towards the door. LADY UNA stops)
Oh, I don't know your name. How strange it is we place so much value on our names, and yet we can manage very well without them. Now child, I hope it's a pleasant one. What do they call you?

EMMA: Emma.

LADY UNA: What did you say?

EMMA: Emma.

LADY UNA: How very unfortunate. I thought I hadn't heard correctly. Oh no. We can't have that. It went out with Nelson.

EMMA: It's the only one I've got. Take it or leave it?

LADY UNA: Not Emmaline nor Emily?

EMMA: Emma.

LADY UNA: Some parents have very little imagination.

EMMA: It's no worse than Bella.

LADY UNA: I agree with you, but I had the sense to change it.

EMMA: Well, I'm not going to change my name.

LADY UNA: We want something that sounds nice, trips off the tongue and harmonises with your personality. Why that's it! The perfect name. Harmony! So attractive. I can see it now in staring red letters at the top of the bill-board. Harmony! Harmony! Harmony! Bring that hideous bag with you. It's quite out of character.

EMMA: Completely scatty.

(She picks up her ruck-sack and follows LADY UNA. BORIS enters stage right. He glares at the opposite fireplace and then getting a chair hangs a large poster over his mirror. It bears the slogan 'Another Victory!' While he is doing this, JEFFERSON enters left and seeing BORIS, creeps stealthily and hides behind a chair on stage left. He watches BORIS and then reaches his telescope and spies round the side of the chair. Meanwhile BORIS has put up the poster and now steps back to admire it. He smiles satisfaction and then shakes his fist at stage left)

BORIS: There.

(JEFFERSON reacts vocally to this. BORIS then gets a pair of binoculars from his mantlepiece and getting down behind his armchair spies on JEFFERSON. They see each other at the same moment and in annoyance rise and, putting their spy glasses back, sit with their backs to each other. Enter LADY UNA and MISS C. carrying papers)

LADY UNA: Do hurry! Do hurry Miss Cowperthwaite. We have so much to do and the situation is deteriorating rapidly.

(She sees the poster, but not BORIS, who is deep in his armchair)

LADY UNA: Look at that. Oh the foolish boy. It's asking for retaliation. Take it down.

MISS C: What, Madam?

LADY UNA: Remove it before Jefferson sees it.

MISS C: But Madam, it's... I should have to cross the hearthrug. If he should come in and see me, he'd... he'd... there is no knowing what he would do.

LADY UNA: I am behind you. We must be prepared to take risks in an emergency. Go along, do as I say.

MISS C: Oh, dear.

(Timorously she crosses right. Just as she is about to set foot on the rug, BORIS jumps up)

BORIS: Get off! Or I'll tear you limb from limb.

(MISS C screams and runs back and hides behind LADY U)

MISS C: Help! Lady Una save me! Save me!

LADY UNA: Boris, behave yourself.

BORIS: I won't have anyone violating my hearthrug.

MISS C: Oh my heart – my heart!

LADY UNA: Pull yourself together Miss Cowperthwaite.

MISS C: I think I'm going to faint.

LADY UNA: Sit down then, loosen something.

(MISS C sinks onto the dais)

LADY UNA: Now Boris, why did you stick that ridiculous poster over your fire-place. It only causes trouble and you know it doesn't mean a thing.

JEFFERSON: *(Jumping up)* Hear! Hear! It is completely untrue, a falsification of the truth.

LADY UNA: Hello, are you here too? Where have you sprung from?

JEFFERSON: I have been here all the time. I've heard everything. It is deliberate provocation.

BORIS: You started it.

JEFFERSON: I didn't.

BORIS: You did.

JEFFERSON: I didn't.

LADY UNA: Silence! This behaviour will get us nowhere. You ought to be ashamed of yourselves. Now Boris, take down that poster at once.

BORIS: No he...

LADY UNA: You heard what I said. At once, I shall use sanctions... no chocolate for you.

(BORIS, like a naughty boy, takes down the poster)

JEFFERSON: *(Advancing to the centre of the room)* Hooray! You see! Truth will prevail!

LADY UNA: Enough! Enough! You have no cause for jubilation.

(BORIS walks deliberately to him)

JEFFERSON: Keep away! Keep away!

(BORIS pulls the poster down over JEFFERSON'S head. LADY U runs down and grabbing each, separates them).

LADY UNA: Now, you'll say you're sorry.

BORIS: I won't.

LADY UNA: Say you're sorry or I'll put you across my knee and spank you, and you know I could do it too. Come along, say you're sorry. I am waiting.

BORIS: Sorry.

JEFFERSON: Ah.

LADY U: And you say you're sorry too.

JEFFERSON: But I haven't done anything.

LADY UNA: *(Shaking him)* Say you're sorry.

JEFFERSON: I'm sorry.

(She releases them)

LADY UNA: It would have been a lot better for both of you if you'd got married and had families. You'd have had someone to think about besides yourselves. Now sit down. I've got something important to tell you.

(They return to their respective chairs)

LADY UNA: I'm going to tell you a story… Perhaps it would be better if you came and sat near me.

(She goes to the throne)

LADY UNA: *(To MISS C)* Have you recovered?

MISS C: It's given me a dreadful headache.

LADY UNA: Then go and get yourself some aspirins.

MISS C: Thank you, Madam.

(She goes to door)

LADY UNA: Don't overdo it. Two are enough.

MISS C: Yes, Madam. *(Exit)*

LADY UNA: Come over here dear boys. There, sit down. The story is a long one.

(They approach and she indicates they should sit at her feet on the dais)

LADY UNA: Are you comfortable? Then I'll begin. Long ago in the depths of a lonely wood there dwelt a basketweaver and his wife. They were very poor, but their poverty did not prevent them from being happy, for they loved each other dearly. This poor couple had one child, a little girl who was the joy of their days and the apple of their eyes. Often when work was scarce, and they had no money to buy food, the father and mother would go without so that their darling child would not starve. Even then, tears of happiness would spring to their eyes as they watched little Harmony, for that was the name they had chosen for their angel, as she played with the pine cones which were the only toys she ever had. One cold winter when the food had been very scarce, the father went to the dark lake wherein grew the reeds with which he made his baskets..Alas, it had been snowing and the poor man, already weak from lack of food, slipping on the frozen ground fell into the lake and drowned.

His wife, not knowing he would never return waited in vain in their tiny little home. Soon there was no food left, and fearful that her darling child would die, clasped her to her bosom and tried to make her way to the nearest village. The snow was deep and a fierce blizzard was blowing. On she struggled but, strong as was her heart, her body was weak and, long before she reached safety, she fell to the ground exhausted. She tried to rise, but her strength had gone. Realising that the angel of death was at hand, the mother covered her innocent child with her cloak and then sheltered it with her body. The morning broke cold but sunny. Alas the mother would never rise again. Miraculously the little child survived and wandered about the countryside finding food and shelter where ever she could, homeless, fatherless, motherless...

(JEFFERSON is sobbing)

Why, Jefferson, you're crying.

BORIS: I'm crying too.

JEFFERSON: That poor child with no one to care for her. I would help her if I could.

BORIS: So would I.

LADY UNA: Excellent. You can both help her. That is not the end of the story. This afternoon a young girl came begging for food at our door. It was Harmony!

JEFFERSON: What, the orphan child?

LADY UNA: The very same.

BORIS: Where is she? Can't we see her?

LADY UNA: You shall. I have a better plan. How would you like to adopt her?

BORIS: Me?

JEFFERSON: No, me.

LADY UNA: Both of you.

BORIS & JEFFERSON: Both of us.

LADY UNA: Yes, you can be her uncles. The uncles she never had...

JEFFERSON: Yes, that's what I've always wanted to do, to help those less fortunate than myself.

BORIS: I haven't noticed it. When can we see her?

JEFFERSON: Is she here now?

BORIS: What is she like?

JEFFERSON: Is she beautiful?

LADY UNA: Don't you think you'd better smarten yourselves up before she sees you?

JEFFERSON: I shall change into my Garden Party suit.

BORIS: I shall wear all my decorations.

LADY UNA: Go and get ready then, and when you return, she will be waiting for you.

JEFFERSON: Yes, yes. I'll go right away.

BORIS: I shall wear my scarlet sash.

(They hurry out by their respective doors. LADY U. sits thinking for a moment and then shouts)

LADY UNA: Rankin! Rankin! Where is the man? Rankin! Oh, there you are.

(The Butler enters)

RANKIN: Madam.

LADY UNA: You know which room we've put the young person in?

RANKIN: The Peacock Room, Madam.

LADY UNA: Yes. Go to her and tell her I am waiting for her.

RANKIN: Yes, Madam.

(He turns to go)

LADY UNA: And, Rankin!

RANKIN: Madam?

LADY UNA: I realise you have flat feet, but can you run?

RANKIN: My feet are a result of my athletic youth, Madam. In my younger days I was a noted athlete and even today, I can for a short distance manage a canter.

LADY UNA: Then do so now!

RANKIN: Yes, Madam.

(He goes quickly)

LADY UNA: On second thoughts, I'd better go myself. Rankin! Rankin! Heaven preserve us, the man whips in and out like a ferret. Rankin I'll go. Rankin!

(At the door she meets MISS C who is just entering)

MISS C: It's better madam.

LADY UNA: Better? Better? What is better?

MISS C: My headache. The aspirins…

LADY UNA: Headaches! Aspirins! There is no time for flippances.

Where's Rankin?... Rankin!

(She runs out shouting and one can hear her receding in the distance. MISS C sits on dias. She is trying to remember the tune of the Charleston and then humming to herself attempts a few steps. RANKIN enters and stands watching her. She sees him and stops self-consciously).

MISS C: I was ...dancing.

RANKIN: Oh, that's what it was.

MISS C: But I'm afraid I'm not very good at it.

RANKIN: No, you're not are you?

MISS C: It's so long since...

RANKIN: There ain't no time for dancing in this house.

MISS C: No... there isn't any time.

RANKIN: Used to be in the old days.

MISS C: In the old days, yes.

RANKIN: Before you came here, that was. When the old man was living. He was a boy, he was. Why we'd have dances here time and time again and everybody welcome. I was hot stuff on dancing myself in those days.

MISS C: Did you... did you dance the Charleston?

RANKIN: Not 'arf. I used to swing 'em round. I was nippy on my feet then.

MISS C: I danced the Charleston too... many years ago. I was trying to remember it, but I'm afraid my memory... and it was such a thrilling dance.

(RANKIN starts humming the Charleston)

MISS C: Yes, that's it. That is the tune.

(She takes it up and they each tentatively try a few steps. Suddenly without realising it, they are dancing the Charleston together. As they dance...)

Oh, it's so gay – so thrilling.

(LADY UNA and EMMA enter. EMMA is now wearing a ribbon and bow in her hair, making her look younger)

LADY UNA: Heaven preserve us! I am no longer young, but while life can furnish sights like this, I shall never be old.

(The dancing stops)

RANKIN: We were dancing, Madam.

LADY UNA: I am relieved to know it was nothing worse. Have you quite finished, Rankin?

RANKIN: Yes, Madam. *(He goes).*

LADY UNA: *(To MISS C)* You are a constant source of surprise to me Miss Cowperthwaite. One minute you are fainting because a man says 'boo' to you and the next I find you gyrating in the arms of the butler.

MISS C: It was the Charleston, Madam.

LADY UNA: Indeed.

EMMA: And very nice too.

MISS C: Thank you, Miss.

LADY UNA: I cannot express an opinion on your Terpsichorean abilities, but don't let me detain you. I am sure Rankin must be wanting to continue the orgy in the butler's pantry. *(MISS C goes)* I think she'll be safe. Now child, let me prepare you to meet your doting uncles.

EMMA: I can't imagine either of them doting over me.

LADY UNA: If you do as I tell you they'll be eating out of your hand. I flatter myself that the picture I painted of you was a little short of a work of genius.

EMMA: Are you sure you haven't made me too beautiful? After all, I'm...

LADY UNA: I never mentioned your looks, so you needn't affect any false modesty, and what I did tell them was a completely fabrication.

EMMA: What have you let me in for?

LADY UNA: When the time came for me to tell them about you, I must confess I was a little non-plussed. Then my memory recalled my own childhood days. I had a little book which was my pride and joy "Tiny tales for tiny tots"; in it was a favourite story which I read over to myself so many times, while mother was busy with her crystal and my father was endeavouring to keep the elephant lines clean. How often I have sat in our overheated caravan reading the story of little Nell, the orphan girl, while tears mingled with my prespiration and dripped off my chin. It was her story with suitable embellishments, which I told your uncles, for you are that orphan child.

EMMA: I'm little orphan Nell?

LADY UNA: You will remember we've changed the name to Harmony. You will be pleased to know that your uncles wept almost as copiously as I used to do. Though I say it myself, my performance was a tour de force. They are ready and anxious to adopt you.

EMMA: And what am I supposed to do?

LADY UNA: You're to be the daughter every father would wish for, the niece every uncle would love, young, sweet and innocent.

EMMA: But I can't do that, I'm not an actress.

LADY UNA: You're a woman. Now let us have no second thoughts.

EMMA: I wouldn't have stayed here if it weren't for that three hundred pounds, which I haven't got and...

LADY UNA: And what?

EMMA: Nothing.

LADY UNA: Now we are wasting time. Remember you are to appeal to both of them. No making more of one than the other. You are here to unite them in a common cause not to stir them to further rivalry. You'd better sit on the stool here, hands crossed on your lap, a sad and wistful expression on your face. Yearning – yearning for love. If you can manage an occasional tear, it will help tremendously. If they ask you any questions, use your native wit, if you haven't any, keep quiet. They'll think it's emotion.

(EMMA sat down in the attitude suggested)

EMMA: Is that all right?

LADY UNA: Beautiful. Turn your toes in a little. That's better. There is something innocent about inturned toes.

EMMA: I feel daft.

LADY UNA: I shall leave you with them, but not for too long for the first time. I believe I can hear Jefferson coming now.

(She crosses to door left and listens)

Yes. Now remember I'm depending on you to restore peace between them. Just let them have a sip, then away with them. Always leave them wanting my dear. Yes, we may get away with it.

(She goes. EMMA sits in her attitude but looks out of the corner of her eyes. JEFFERSON peeps in and seeing EMMA, spruces himself and then advances to her left. She doesn't move and after a moment he speaks)

JEFFERSON: Excuse me.

EMMA: Oh Sir, how you startled me.

JEFFERSON: I am sorry, I didn't intend to.Charming, charming. I am Jefferson.

EMMA: Mr Jefferson.

JEFFERSON: You look half-starved.

EMMA: Do I?

JEFFERSON: But very charming.

EMMA: Oh.

JEFFERSON: I have brought you a present.

EMMA: Oh.

JEFFERSON: Guess what it is.

EMMA: Please sir, I can't.

JEFFERSON: It's something very nice, something you'll like... Make a guess.

EMMA: It's a..a..

JEFFERSON: Yes.

EMMA: A golden bracelet.

JEFFERSON: Better than that.

EMMA: A diamond necklace.

JEFFERSON: No... It's a cream puff
(He produces it from behind his back)

EMMA: Oh *(Taking it)* thank you.

JEFFERSON: You must be very hungry after all your wanderings.

EMMA: *(Eating)* I certainly am. I haven't had a decent meal since...

JEFFERSON: I know, since your poor mother died in the snow.

EMMA: She..? Oh yes, my poor mother.

JEFFERSON: Lady Una told me all about your terrible experience... It was a miracle... a miracle.

EMMA: It must have been.

JEFFERSON: I want to know... I want to... I would like...

EMMA: Yes?

JEFFERSON: Do you think you could accept me... I mean... Do you think you could like me?

EMMA: You're like the uncle I've always imagined... always wanted.

JEFFERSON: I am? But this is wonderful. Why it's just what I was going to suggest. I shall be your Uncle Jefferson.

EMMA: Uncle Jefferson.

JEFFERSON: You can call me Uncle Jeffy if you'd rather.

EMMA: Thank you... Uncle Jeffy.

JEFFERSON: Then you will be my niece?

EMMA: Yes.

JEFFERSON: Oh, thank you. Oh I'm so happy. Oh I'm so happy... would you like a diamond necklace?

EMMA: With an emerald pendant.

JEFFERSON: You shall have one. I know your name. Lady Una told it to me... Harmony... Harmony!

EMMA: Yes, Uncle Jeffy.

JEFFERSON: Will you let me kiss you?

EMMA: What! Well just one.

JEFFERSON: Thank you.

> *(She offers her cheek and he is kissing it when BORIS enters. BORIS reacts).*

BORIS: Oh, what's this? What's this? What's this?

JEFFERSON: I'm her uncle.

BORIS: So am I.

JEFFERSON: Ah, but she's said I can be her uncle. Haven't you Harmony?

BORIS: This is taking an unfair advantage. It's just what I might have expected. Robber. Thief. Letcher.

EMMA: Oh, I doubt it. You mustn't shout at Uncle Jeffy like that.

BORIS: Uncle Jeffy!

EMMA: Only because he met me first. But I can call you Uncle too, if you like.

BORIS: Of course you must.

EMMA: But first you must say you're sorry to Uncle Jeffy.

BORIS: What for.

EMMA: For calling him those nasty names.

BORIS: You should hear all the things he says about me.

EMMA: When I do, he'll have to apologise too. I can't have Uncles talking like that. It's not nice, particularly in front of an innocent girl.

BORIS: What do you want me to do?

EMMA: Say you're sorry.

BORIS: I'm sorry. Now am I your uncle?

EMMA: Yes, if you behave nicely.

BORIS: Uncle Boris.

EMMA: Now I've got two uncles. Uncle Jefferson and Uncle Boris.

BORIS: You let him kiss you.

> *(She puts out her cheek and he kisses her and glares at JEFFERSON)*

EMMA: Uncle Jefferson is going to give me a diamond necklace.

JEFFERSON: And she's worth it.

BORIS: I'll give you a diamond necklace set with sapphires.

EMMA: But, I don't want two. I've only one neck Uncle Boris.

> *(She giggles)*

BORIS: You can have whatever you like, my dear. Just say what you want and Uncle Boris will get it for you.

EMMA: I'll try to think of something good. It's no use spoiling the ship...

BORIS: Yes, whatever you like.

(He tries to kiss her again)

EMMA: Now, now.

BORIS: What's the matter?

EMMA: You have had one kiss, Oh dear.

BORIS: Are you ill?

EMMA: Auntie Una said you musn't stay too long because I'm weak and tired.

JEFFERSON: It's all that wandering in the woods.

BORIS: We'll soon have you fit and well.

EMMA: So, perhaps you'd better go now.

JEFFERSON & BORIS: Oh!... already?

BORIS: I've only just got here.

EMMA: You may kiss me before you go. Both of you.

(They both go to kiss her)

EMMA: *(Pointing to her cheeks)* Wait! There Uncle Jefferson and you there, Uncle Boris.

(They both kiss her)

JEFFERSON: Bye, bye, Harmony, see you again.

BORIS: See you again Harmony dear. Bye, bye.

(They glare at each other and go to door. Each stops at the door and waves)

JEFFERSON & BORIS: Bye, bye!

(They go. EMMA trips over to the mirror and straightens her bow. She then returns to throne, but sees TONI who is standing in the doorway left. She looks the other way and sits with her back to him. He enters).

TONI: You don't look very weak to me. What are you wearing that bow for?

(He indicates the bow)

(No answer)

I don't think it suits you.

(No answer)

Still I suppose Uncle Boris and Uncle Jeffy like it.

EMMA: You've been listening?

TONI: Yes.

EMMA: That's a nice way to behave isn't it? A gentleman doesn't listen at doors.

TONI: I'm only a servant. Uncle Jeffy and Uncle Boris are gentlemen.

EMMA: Stop saying that like that.

TONI: Saying what like what?

EMMA: You know what I mean. Uncle Jeffy and Uncle Boris.

TONI: But that's what you call them.

EMMA: It's part of my job.

TONI: What is your job?

EMMA: Never mind.

(Pause)

Well? What did you want to talk about?

TONI: Nothing.

EMMA: Not much use staying then.

TONI: Are you hungry?

EMMA: No.

TONI: I'll bet you are. I'll bet you wish you'd eaten some of that food I brought you.

EMMA: No, I don't.

TONI: I'll get you some if you like.

EMMA: I'm not hungry, thank you.

TONI: Sure you wouldn't like some chicken sandwiches?

EMMA: *(Wavering at last)* Er...no.

TONI: That's all right then. I thought perhaps you were hungry.

(He turns to go. She stops him)

EMMA: Er...Toni

TONI: Yes?

EMMA: Where are they? The chicken sandwiches?

TONI: Just outside in the kitchen. They'll only be thrown away.

EMMA: What a waste.

TONI: Yes.

EMMA: All right... rather than waste them.

TONI: How many?

EMMA: Six.

TONI: Six?

EMMA: Seven.

(He gives her a look and goes. She takes the ribbon out of her hair and crossing to the mirror, attends to her hair and applies lipstick. She scurries back to the throne just as he enters with sandwiches)

TONI: Here you are.

(She takes sandwiches. He sits on dais).

EMMA: Thank you.

TONI: You don't mind if I sit here do you?

EMMA: No.

(Offering sandwiches) Want one-

TONI: I only brought seven.

EMMA: I can make do with six. Here.

TONI: *(Taking sandwiches)* Thanks.

(They sit eating in silence. She has joined him on the dais).

EMMA: Hmmm. Nice.

TONI: You've taken off your ribbon.

EMMA: It came undone.

TONI: You were right.

EMMA: What about?

TONI: I can't get you out of my mind.

EMMA: Good.

TONI: No, it isn't. Why should I have to come in here and talk to you and run about bringing you sandwiches and things?

EMMA: I didn't ask you to and the sandwiches were your suggestion.

TONI: You're glad I suggested them.

EMMA: Of course. I love chicken.

(Pause)

TONI: Why have you come here?

EMMA: I was kidnapped. Had you anything to do with it?

TONI: Why should I want to kidnap you?

EMMA: Charming, aren't you?

TONI: How long are you going to stay?

EMMA: Don't know. It depends.

TONI: What does it depend on?

EMMA: You're very young aren't you?

TONI: I'm twenty-four. How old are you?

EMMA: I'm just about the right age I think.. don't you?

TONI: Why do you look at me like that? You're trying to disturb me again. You're turning everything upside down and I can't think properly and... Oh.

EMMA: Go on. Don't stop now, please.

TONI: No. No. I'm going back to my room.

EMMA: Well, if you're not the most frustrating man I've ever struck.

TONI: But I shan't be free of you I know that. You'll still be there and you'll make me think about you, even if I don't want to. You can do that can't you?

EMMA: Yes I can.

TONI: Are you a witch?

EMMA: What do you think.

TONI: You've put a spell on me.

EMMA: I've got something for you.

TONI: What?

EMMA: Wait till I've finished this sandwich. There, now Toni my
     darling, come here.
     (He comes slowly towards her)

EMMA: Kiss me.

TONI: No...

EMMA: Come on, kiss me.
     (He is about to kiss her cheek)

EMMA: That's reserved for Uncles.
     *(She puts her lips temptingly and he kisses her and with very little
     more persuasion from her, takes her in his arms).*

END OF ACT 2

ACT 3   SCENE ONE

(Action continues)
(It has been a long kiss. She releases him and he stands looking at her for a moment then moves away)

EMMA: Phew! That was quite an effort. You've got possibilities.
(No answer)
Did you like it?

TONI: No!

EMMA: Liar! Try again.

TONI: No, no. You are a witch. Only a witch could have made me do that.

EMMA: Don't be silly. All I did was kiss you as heartily as you kissed me, and you ought to feel jolly pleased about it.

TONI: You've made me weak. I'm shaking all over. I was strong before, but now my knees are all jelly and I'm hot and cold and ...oh!

EMMA: I must be pretty good. It'll soon pass my little Toni, and you'll be stronger than ever and you'll come back for more.

TONI: Oh no, I shan't, never again.

EMMA: You won't be able to help yourself.

TONI: You see. You're a witch and yet you don't look evil to me.

EMMA: What do I look like to you, Toni.

TONI: No! Leave me alone. Why must you torment me like this? Before you came I was happy and contented but now you've done this to me, I don't know what's going to happen.

EMMA: Isn't it thrilling?

TONI: No, it isn't. I'm afraid. I don't know what's going to happen next. I always knew what I was going to do every day.

EMMA: How boring.

TONI: No, it wasn't. I was happy. I knew where I was, but now I don't know where I am. Anything can happen and nothing will be certain again. I don't know anything.

EMMA: But you'll learn. Now you've really awakened, and this very morning will be the beginning of a journey. A voyage of discovery. You'll see everthing for the first time; you'll be living and that's worth all the risk of disappointment.

TONI: You've made me want something and I don't know what I want. Why have you done this to me?

EMMA: I don't know.

TONI: I don't suppose you care either.

EMMA: Oh yes I care, but I don't know why any more than you. It's a terrible thing, sex, isn't it? Why should it be you and me? We don't know, we only know that it is. You've cast a spell over me as I've cast one over you... Toni!

TONI: Yes?

(EMMA puts her lips for a kiss. He hesitates, gives her a sharp kiss and then runs from the room).

TONI: No, no no.

(At the door he almost bowles over LADY UNA who is entering. He goes).

LADY UNA: That young man appears to be in a great hurry. What have you been doing to him my dear child?

EMMA: He makes me sick.

LADY UNA: Indeed? I should have thought? by the speed of his disappearance, that he was the one who had taken an emetic. You haven't had occasion to box his ears have you?

EMMA: No.

LADY UNA: It is all very strange. With his virility and your youthfulness, I should have expected him to be charging in and not out. I can't imagine human nature has changed since I was a girl. But to business.

EMMA: Oh lor!

LADY UNA: You appear to be in a mood. That we can't have. You have your contract to fulfil and remember, whatever your private feelings may be, the show must go on.

EMMA: I wish you'd stop talking like a third-rate musical comedy producer. If I don't feel like it, there won't be any show and at the moment I never felt less like being a sweet innocent young orphan, so there.

LADY UNA: Dear, dear, dear, you are in a mood. I think I recognize it too. It's that boy. Is he being difficult?

(EMMA tosses her head)

Oh, you can toss your head, but I'll wager that I'm right, and I don't wonder you're piqued about it either. When I was your age, I would guarantee to turn the head of a press agent, let alone a healthy youngster who's never met a girl in his life before. No man ever ran away from me unless I wanted him to. It's unthinkable.

EMMA: Have you quite finished?

LADY UNA: Indeed I haven't. It's my conviction that this militant approach you moderns have is all wrong. You women are too manly to be womanly. All this grabbing a man by the scruff of the neck and shaking him into submission. It won't do. It's enough to ruin him for life. When I was young, we used to wait for them to come to us, not chase after them. But we made sure they came. They thought they had caught us. We knew we had caught them. Honour was satisfied and a good time was had by all... invariably. And now, having said that, we will get back to business. Revenons a nos moutons as the stage manager at the Follies used to say. You saw your uncles? I trust you were successfully demure?

EMMA: If you mean did they accept me as orphan Annie, the answer is yes. They are now my uncles and I'm their niece and now what about the three hundred pounds?

LADY UNA: My dear child, what a time to ask such a question. How very unromantic.

EMMA: I'm only following your advice and incidentally, that's all you have given me so far, advice.

LADY UNA: An oversight, my dear, an oversight. I have asked Miss Cowperthwaite to make out a cheque for you. I trust that will be in order?

EMMA: Yes, as long as it doesn't bounce.

LADY UNA: That's rather a vulgar suggestion, my dear. But tell me more of your uncles. I trust they agreed to share you jointly. You were perfectly impartial I hope.

EMMA: Perfectly. They even kissed me together.

LADY UNA: Excellent! Excellent! They kissed you? You're going to earn your money child, I can see. But your hair ribbon... where is it? You haven't been giving favours to one and not the other have you?

EMMA: No, it's here. I took it off after they'd gone.

LADY UNA: Ah well. It's served its purpose. Now I have worked out the next move. We must have a reception for you.

EMMA: It's a bit late for that, isn't it?

LADY UNA: This is to be the official reception. With full formality and regalia. Jefferson and Boris will be delighted. They love dressing up. To be honest I rather enjoy it myself. I always think I cut quite a figure in my Edwardian gown.

EMMA: Edwardian!

LADY UNA: It is so dignified, feminine and quite irreproachable. You'll be pleased to know I have found the thing for you. It is the costume I wore for my first appearance as a solo act. I was only fourteen at the time and I should say about your size. A charming costume in virgin white with spangles and tights.

EMMA: Oh no!

LADY UNA: Oh indeed yes. It's the very thing. You'll look like the fairy off the Christmas tree. I wish I could wear it again, but alas the heart is willing but the flesh is too much. And you won't have to wear that ribbon either. There's a beautiful tinsel crown. But come along, you shall try it on now. It may need a few alterations here and there.

(They go)

(BORIS enters right. He looks to make sure the room is empty and then crosses to the fire right. He looks suspiciously and then takes out a balloon. He is about to blow it up when JEFFERSON enters left).

(BORIS puts the balloon away hurriedly and pretends indifference. JEFFERSON opens a newspaper and peeps from behind it. BORIS goes out and returns with a screen which he places between him and JEFFERSON. Behind it, he begins to blow up the balloon and tie it).

(JEFFERSON, hearing him blow, creeps across the room to the screen and listens. BORIS suspecting, peers round screen behind him)

BORIS: Ah!

(JEFFERSON leaps and retreats rapidly to his own hearthrug. BORIS follows him to centre)

JEFFERSON: No, no.

BORIS: Spy! Criminal! Saboteur!

JEFFERSON: I'm not! I'm not! I was tying my shoelace.

BORIS: Liar! You were spying on me. You were encroaching on my territory.

JEFFERSON: I wasn't on your hearthrug.

BORIS: You were within three feet of it. I've told you before, I won't have you spying on me.

JEFFERSON: If you've nothing to be ashamed of, why do you hide behind a screen?

BORIS: That's my secret, and I'm going to keep it a secret.

JEFFERSON: You're planning something aren't you? Your planning something against me.

BORIS: Are you afraid?

JEFFERSON: Of you? No, I'm not. I'm not afraid of you. I'm ready for anything. You're not the only one with plans. I am prepared.

BORIS: Prepared for what?

JEFFERSON: For defence.

BORIS: Pooh!

JEFFERSON: And pooh to you.

BORIS: I shall report your behaviour to Lady Una.
    (Enter LADY UNA)

LADY UNA: And what will you report to Lady Una?

BORIS: He's been spying on me.

JEFFERSON: Lies, all lies.   *(Spoken together)*

BORIS: He's been trying to discover my secret.

JEFFERSON: He's plotting against me.

BORIS: Thief.

JEFFERSON: Dog!

BORIS: Viper!

JEFFERSON: Murderer!

LADY UNA: Silence! Silence! Silence! I have told you before I will listen to you one at a time, but not when you come shouting and bawling together... now then...

BORIS: He came...   )

JEFFERSON: He said...)

LADY UNA: One at a time please! Now Jefferson, what have you to say?

BORIS: I protest! I protest! It's my turn to speak first. He spoke first last time.

LADY UNA: What does it matter who speaks first. If he speaks first, you'll have the last say.

BORIS: It's a matter of procedure... a question of principle.

LADY UNA: Very well then, you speak first.

JEFFERSON: I protest. You have already called on me to speak.

LADY UNA: I won't listen to either of you. You're behaving like naughty little children and I'm not at all sure that I will tell you about the lovely surprise I've arranged for you now.

JEFFERSON: A lovely surprise. What is it?

BORIS: I'm not interested.

LADY UNA: What do you think your new niece would say if she saw you behaving like this? You ought to be ashamed of yourselves.

BORIS: I demand that my protest shall by heard.

LADY UNA: Very well. Make your protest and be done.

BORIS: Ten minutes ago, my brother Jefferson was observed by me, creeping on my territory with the obvious intention of spying on me while engaged on highly secret work.

LADY UNA: What were you doing?

JEFFERSON: He was plotting against me

LADY UNA: Silence!

BORIS: I protest. I was not plotting against anyone. My intentions are strictly peaceful.

LADY UNA: What were you doing?

BORIS: I protest. You have no right to ask me that question. My secrets are secret; but this I will say, soon you will know, everyone will know, that I, Boris, have succeeded, that my achievements have far surpassed anything yet conceived by anyone else.

JEFFERSON: You see! You see! You see! He's causing trouble again.

(Enter MISS COWPERTHWAITE)

MISS C: Lady Una! Lady Una! Oh, I'm sorry I didn't know...

LADY UNA: What is it Miss Cowperthwaite?

MISS C: All right Madam. I can wait. I can wait.

LADY UNA: This really is getting too much for me.

(Shouting) What is it you want to say Miss Cowperthwaite?

MISS C: Oh yes...yes...well it isn't me really. It's the young person, Madam.

LADY UNA: Well?

MISS C: She wants to know if you can come at once, Madam. It's urgent.

LADY UNA: Why? What is the matter?

MISS C: She's split her tights, Madam!

LADY UNA: Heaven preserve us.

JEFFERSON: Tights? Tights! What's that? Who's split her tights?

LADY UNA: Control yourself Jefferson, control yourself.

BORIS: Do I understand you to say that my niece, my poor, darling niece, is being tricked out in tights?

LADY UNA: I wish you would have a little more tact Miss Cowperthwaite. Now I shall have to tell them everything. My dear boys, this is part of the lovely surprise I am preparing for you. Your little niece, Harmony, is really a fairy.

JEFFERSON: A fairy? A real fairy?

BORIS: I don't believe in fairies. They're decadent.

JEFFERSON: In that case, I do believe in fairies, I shall have her all to myself. Eh! Eh! Eh!

BORIS: I protest.

LADY UNA: Silence! Now listen carefully. Tonight there is to be an official banquet and reception in her honour.

JEFFERSON: Hoorah!

LADY UNA: Full uniform and decorations will be worn and I trust that everyone will attend.

JEFFERSON: Goody goody. I shall wear my purple pinny.

BORIS: I shall wear the order of the fork and trowel, first class, with lettuce leaves.

LADY UNA: Excellent.

MISS C: Do you think it would be the thing for me to wear my Charleston tea-gown?

LADY UNA: It is permissable, but whether it will be the thing is a matter of opinion.

JEFFERSON: Tonight I shall give her the diamond necklace.
(He bows and goes out)

BORIS: Tonight, I shall amaze everyone. In her honour I shall demonstrate my greatest, my most stupendous achievement! The world will be staggered.
(He salutes and exits)

LADY UNA: It would appear, Miss Cowperthwaite that tonight is going to be quite an occasion. Come let us attend to the tights.
(She goes)

End of Act 3 Scene 1

ACT 3   SCENE TWO

One hour later
(A long table has been set below the dais. On it decorations etc., 4
upright candelabra. RANKIN and TONI are laying crockery and
cutlery from a dumb waiter. The room has been decorated with
festoons etc.)

RANKIN: Official reception and banquet. Did you ever hear such
twaddle? Anyone would think Royalty had arrived. Who is she?
I'd like to know. Who is she to have all this palaver made over her?

TONI: She's...

RANKIN: I know who she is, and put those knives straight. It's
unlucky to have crossed knives. She's a common little hiker I
picked up on the road outside.

TONI: I don't think she's common.

RANKIN: You don't think she's common! You don't think she's
common! And how are you to know whether she's common or
not. What exeeperience have you had. Have you seen her?

TONI: Yes, I've seen her and she seemed very uncommon to me.

RANKIN: Oh, she did, did she? Well I found her. I brought her in
and I'm telling you my lad, she's common, and now what happens?
She's treated like a blinking V.I.P. She calls the two old gents
uncle, her ladyship re-christens her Harmony – Harmony! – and
we've got to do all this extra work.

TONI: I don't suppose she asked for this banquet. She can't be
hungry.

RANKIN: It makes no difference whether she asked for it or not, she's getting it, and we've got to do the work. But, I'll tell you something my lad. They're going to be disappointed. You should have seen the menu her ladyship sent down to the kitchen. Long as your flippin' arm. And d'you know what they're getting? Cold sausages and blancmange. Old Boris has been tinkering with the gas pipes or something. Couldn't get a glimmer in the kitchens.

TONI: Then why are we laying all these things?

RANKIN: Appearances. Her ladyship has ordered a banquet, so it's got to look like a banquet, even if there's nothing to eat.

TONI: But it's so ridiculous...

RANKIN: My boy, when you've had my experience you'll realise that a lot of things that are done in the upper circle are just plain bloody silly. It's always been like that, and it always will be.

TONI: But, why do they do it?

RANKIN: Helps them to feel important. They could make their speeches just as well over a plate of fish and chips, but you won't catch 'em doing that.

TONI: Well I don't mind working if there's something to work for. I wouldn't mind preparing for a banquet if they were going to have one, but I see no sense at all in laying all these knives and forks and things if they are not going to be used.

RANKIN: That's enough. That's fighting talk. Revolutionary. It's not for you or me to say what should be done or what shouldn't be done. We're the workers. We do what we're told. Oh I know that nowadays, there's a tendency to ask us rather than to order us, but it only comes to the same thing in the end, and we've got to do it.

TONI: Why?

RANKIN: We've got to live. In the old days I didn't mind so much. The governor was more than a bit crackers, but he had something. He'd been sort of born to it. You felt, somehow, he had the right to boss you about. But, these days, we've got flippin' circus queens running the show and the nicer they are, the more I resent it. Funny but it's true – and I'll tell you something else too. They're just as crackers as the old lot without the breedin'.

(He picks up a fish knife, examines it, wipes it on the seat of his pants and then being satisfied with its appearance, replaces it)

No, we're here. We have our jobs and we might as well stay in them, because if we went anywhere else, it would be just the same, if not worse. I won't say I'm contented, I'm just resigned...

philosophically resigned.

TONI: Well, I'm not. I've never heard you talk like this before.

RANKIN: I've thought it, but today I'm in the mood to speak out. This girl coming here has upset me, I don't mind telling you.

TONI: She's upset me, too.

RANKIN: What d'you mean? Here, you've not been smelling around there have you?

TONI: I don't know what it is. I've never felt the same since I met her. Is that how she affects you?

RANKIN: Me! At my age? It's the principle of the thing. All this fuss for somebody who's done nothing to deserve it. But you must be careful, son. These woman can make a mess of your life if you don't watch out. I know. I've had some. What's she been saying to you?

TONI: It isn't what she says. It's the way she looks at me and the things she does.

RANKIN: Here, this is getting serious. What's she done? And what d'you mean? The way she looks at you?

TONI: Well...as though she can see right through inside...

RANKIN: I know.. they're devils that sort and.. what did she do?

TONI: She made me kiss her.

RANKIN: D'you mean she asked you to?

TONI: No... she ordered me.

RANKIN: Crikey! I've never met one like that. You'd better keep out of the house while she's here.

TONI: I tried to.. but I couldn't. She made me come in. Do you think she's a witch?

RANKIN: All women are witches. If there's something they want they'll get it and they don't care what they do to get it either. Look at the suffragettes. That was before your time my lad. Votes for women they wanted and votes for women they were going to get. They talked and spouted, argued, and fought.. no use.. so they decided to suffer.. got themselves clapped in gaol. Nobody liked them while they were fighting like hell-cats, so they switched to the old "weaker sex" angle and that was it boy. All men were blood-thirsty brutes and bullies. That's why there are wars. So they gave them the vote and since then we've had the two bloodiest wars there's ever been.

TONI: You can't blame only the women. Everybody's crazy. Look at this place. What use is it laying a table when there's nothing to eat. It's a waste of time. I think I'll look for another job.

RANKIN: Pipe down lad. It won't make no difference. All jobs are the same.. and look out, here's the Duchess.

(Enter LADY UNA in her Edwardian gown)

That will be all boy, take the waiter back to the kitchen.

(TONI takes the dumb waiter out)

LADY UNA: Everything prepared for the banquet, Rankin?

RANKIN: Yes, Madam.

LADY UNA: *(Surveying table)* Let me see, yes very charming. I think nothing looks nicer or more exciting than a well-laid table. It's a great pity we are limited to sausages and blancmange. However, we shall proceed as though nothing was wrong. With all the excitement, the singularly uninteresting nature of the food will pass unnoticed.

RANKIN: We can only hope so, Madam.

LADY UNA: I shall sit in the centre of course, with the girl on my right and Miss Cowperthwaite on my left. Boris and Jefferson will take their respective ends of the table. Do you realise Rankin, this is the first banquet we've had since I've been here. I expect you had many such events in the old days.

RANKIN: Indeed yes, Madam. The old master was a great one for entertaining.

LADY UNA: I should like to do more myself, but this is the first time we've been able to find a guest who was equally acceptable to both Boris and Jefferson. I'm... Good heavens, what's happened now? *(The lights have failed suddenly and save for the red glow from the two fireplaces and the moonlight through the windows, the room is in darkness)*

RANKIN: It would appear, Madam, that the lighting system has failed.

LADY UNA: That is a very obvious remark, Rankin. The point is why has it failed and at this particular moment. Light the candles. What was good enough for our fore-fathers, will have to serve us. It's a remarkable fact that with all our planning, Austerity still lurks around the corner.

(The butler lights the candles)

It would seem that everything is conspiring against my arrangements.

Well, they shall not prevent me from going ahead. I have learned in the hard school that nothing must stand in the way of the performance. The banquet will commence at the appointed time. I'm not at all sure that this candle-light is not an improvement. It is unexpected, it gives an atmosphere and Boris and Jefferson won't be able to see each other as distinctly. That is always an advantage.. Ah Miss Cowperthwaite..

(Enter MISS COWPERTHWAITE in her Charleston tea gown...)

No!... I wouldn't have believed it possible.

MISS C: What Lady Una?

LADY UNA: Those legs. I suppose they must belong to you, but it is inconceivable that you should want anyone to know.

MISS C: This is my Charleston tea gown, Madam. It takes me back thirty years. Ah! Those were happy, carefree days.

(She begins to hum the Charleston)

LADY UNA: Miss Cowperthwaite, I may be tone-deaf, but that does not give you permission to inflict your vocal efforts on me. I presume you had a reason for coming to see me.

MISS C: Oh yes, Madam. It's Miss Harmony. She's ready, and Madam, she looks charming. Positively charming. She wants to know if it is all right to come down.

LADY UNA: We're waiting for her. Tell her to come at once. It is almost time for the reception.

MISS C: Yes, Madam.

(She goes)

LADY UNA: Rankin, you'd better sound the gong. The meal will be served immediately Mr Boris and Mr Jefferson are here.

RANKIN: Certainly, Madam.

(He goes. LADY UNA moves around the table putting an occasional knife straight and smelling the flowers. The gong is heard off and at the same time EMMA appears in the doorway left. She is in a white ballet dress and wears a tinsel crown. MISS C hovers in the background carrying a lamp)

EMMA: Will I pass?

LADY UNA: Charming! Completely charming! For once Miss Cowperthwaite you were right.

EMMA: I feel like something out of a pantomime.

LADY UNA: And why not? What is more charming than panto-mime? If the modern generation feels itself too sophisticated to enjoy pantomime, then it is to be pitied. Come closer. You almost make me weep. It is as though I looked into a mirror and saw myself as I was, I won't say how many years ago.

(She puts the crown a shade straighter) That's better.

EMMA: I couldn't see to get dressed properly. What's happened to the electricity?

LADY UNA: I don't know, but we are not letting it affect us. This candle light is as becoming to youth as it is to age. Now dear, you will sit on my right and Miss Cowperthwaite on my left. But listen! It sounds as if your uncles are coming. Come with me.

(LADY UNA goes to the throne and sits with EMMA standing on her right. A fanfare on a tin trumpet is heard off right. Enter BORIS and JEFFERSON through respective doors)

LADY UNA: Greetings.

BORIS & JEFFERSON: Greetings Lady Una and to our niece.

LADY U: Thank you. And now we will take our places.

(Shouting) Rankin! The wine.

(They sit at the table in their respective places. RANKIN enters with the wine and pours into each glass. EMMA is wriggling)

LADY UNA: Stop wriggling my dear.

EMMA: It's all right for you. You've got a bustle. This chair's darn cold.

LADY U: You can't have it all ways, child. And now I ask you to raise your glasses and drink to our new niece to our charming little fairy, Harmony.

(They all rise and drink the toast)

ALL: Harmony!

(MISS COWPERTHWAITE begins to cough)

LADY UNA: Miss Cowperthwaite please! Anyone would think you'd never tasted wine before.

MISS C: I'm sorry Madam. It was stronger than I expected.

(BORIS and JEFFERSON rise together)

BORIS: I would like...

JEFFERSON: I am delighted.

(They stop and glare at each other)

LADY UNA: One at a time please!

(They are both about to start again but she forstalls them)

Now, we can't have any petty arguments on an occasion like this. Jefferson, you speak first and Boris you will follow.

(JEFFERSON smiles his triumph and BORIS sulks)

BORIS: I protest.

LADY UNA: Oh, not again. Your protestations are becoming monotonous.

BORIS: I am sure my niece will take note that once again preference is being given to the other side. It grieves me to have to take action on such an occasion, but I know that Harmony will agree with me that this is a matter which cannot be allowed to pass unchallenged. It is no reflection on you, my dear, but I must leave this gathering in protest. It is the only course left to me. Before I go, however, I shall make an announcement of great importance. I have long been experimenting with gas-filled balloons and my experiments have, at last, met with complete success. Tonight as a mark of honour to my darling niece, I shall release the greatest fleet of gas-filled balloons ever to be seen... Long live Boris.

JEFFERSON: Ha, ha, ha. Balloons! Lovely little balloons! Baby-house.

(BORIS picks up a sausage and throws it at JEFFERSON)

JEFFERSON: Aggression! Unprovoked agression!

EMMA: Oh, for pity's sake.

JEFFERSON: He threw a sausage at me.

LADY UNA: Boris, go to your room at once. Your behaviour lacks dignity.

BORIS: Dignity! Pooh!

(BORIS pulls the tablecloth and its contents with a crash to the floor and marches out. MISS COWPERTHWAITE screams. General consternation)

LADY UNA: Rankin! Rankin! Help! Where are you?

RANKIN: *(Going to door)* Toni! Toni!

LADY UNA: Clear away this mess.

MISS C: Oh my dress, my dress.

LADY U: Oh shut up.

(To HARMONY) Are you all right my dear?

EMMA: I'm just beginning to enjoy myself.

LADY UNA: Indeed! Wrap it in the cloth Rankin. Miss Cowper-thwaite this is not the end of the world.

(TONI has entered)

RANKIN: *(To TONI)* Help me to clear this.

JEFFERSON: I declare a state of emergency. Our future is in the melting pot. We are balanced on a knife edge.

LADY UNA: This is no time for rhetoric. Haven't you finished yet, Rankin?

RANKIN: Yes, Madam.

(He goes out with debris in the cloth. TONI follow him)

LADY UNA: Sometimes, I almost despair. However we will try to proceed as though nothing had happened. Jefferson, I believe you were about to make a speech of welcome.

JEFFERSON: Now?

Oh, very well. This is a most auspicious occasion. I have always grieved that I have never had any children. No loved ones to cluster at my knee, but now all is changed. Suddenly a fairy has appeared, a beautiful white fairy and, miracle of miracles, that fairy has become my niece. I am deeply moved. I am very touched and, at the same time, very happy.

LADY UNA: Cut it short.

JEFFERSON: I beg your pardon madam?

LADY UNA: I am sitting in a pool of sauterne.

JEFFERSON: Oh, I see. I could not let such an occasion pass without giving some tangible expression of my pleasure and my love. I ask you then, my dear Harmony, to accept this little necklace from your Uncle Jeffy. May I?

(He goes to EMMA and fastens a diamond necklace round her neck)

LADY UNA: Sparklers! You've touched lucky my girl.

MISS C: Oh, how beautiful. How beautiful.

EMMA: Oh, thank you, Uncle Jeffy.

(She offers her cheek to be kissed. At that moment there is an explosion off, as though a balloon had burst)

JEFFERSON: What's that? What's that? What is he up to?

(He runs to the fireplace, grabs his telescope and running to window, looks out)

LADY UNA: Control yourself, Jefferson.

JEFFERSON: By gad, he's done it. He's done it! Hundreds, thousands of balloons swirling up into the sky. This is most humiliating to me. I must take counter-measures immediately.

(He hurries out. MISS C runs to the window)

MISS C: Balloons? Balloons? Oh yes, there they are...

LADY UNA: Miss Cowperthwaite.

MISS C: But, Madam, do come and look...

LADY UNA: Miss Cowperthwaite! If the male members of this establishment choose to behave in a manner more suited to kindergarten, it is no reason for you to behave likewise.

MISS C: Oh, Madam, they're beautiful, soaring up to heaven like.. like.. so many moons, higher and higher blue moons, red moons, golden moons. May I go into the garden to get a better view?

LADY UNA: Go, go, go, if you must. Anything is better than that ecstatic gurgling.

MISS C: Thank you. Thank you. I've always loved balloons...

(MISS C has run out. EMMA has run across to the mirror to admire the necklace. LADY U sits in the lonely state)

EMMA: *(At mirror)* They're beautiful.

LADY UNA: This is the first banquet I have ever organized. I would scarcely describe it as an unqualified success. The only satisfaction is that I shall not now be forced to eat those sausages.

(There is a loud bang outside, followed by many others as though a pyrotechnic display was being given)

LADY UNA: Lord have mercy on us. What's happening now?

(She goes to the left window and EMMA runs to the other. The fireworks continue to explode.

EMMA: It's a firework display! Hooray! Look, that rocket has just hit a balloon.

LADY UNA: Oh dear. Oh dear, those boys, they're completely ungovernable. I ought to have guessed, I should have stopped him.

EMMA: But what is it? What's happening?

LADY UNA: Jefferson is firing rockets at Boris's balloons. Jealousy, jealousy and envy. They don't think, they don't care what it may lead to. *(MISS C comes running in, in terror)*

MISS C: Madam, the house is on fire. The rockets have set the house on fire.

LADY UNA: Nonsense, pull yourself together. It's only a firework display.

MISS C: It isn't! It isn't! Help! Help! Help!

(She runs out screaming)

EMMA: It does look as though there are flames...

LADY UNA: This inflamatory atmosphere is infectious. No sooner does one person show signs of becoming unbalanced than everyone else follows suit. People are dashing about shouting treachery! Murder! Fire! Or whatever may be the prevailing scare, without knowing whither they're going nor why. Now, I've discovered there is only one thing to do at a moment like this. Nothing. One must relax, stand still and if one does, the whole thing dies down and very little will have happened. I shall do what I always do. I shall play my 'cello.

(She sits on the throne and takes up her 'cello)
In the midst of all this uncertainty and fear how soothing music is.
Switch on the gramophone, child. The record is already in position
and I cannot wait to play.

EMMA: But you can't play…

LADY UNA: I can. I can. Start it at once.. the little black disc.

EMMA: The electricity has failed. The gramophone won't start.

LADY UNA: I am waiting. I am waiting. Hurry. See, my bow is
poised. Switch on!

EMMA: Oh, very well. There.. you see. It doesn't work.
*(She switches on the gramophone. It does not work, but LADY
UNA begins to bow and the music of "La Cygne" can be heard)*

LADY UNA: Ah beautiful.. beautiful..

EMMA: But Lady Una…

LADY UNA: Silence, child. Have you no ear for the music?

EMMA: Oh I can hear and it's beautiful, but the record isn't playing.

LADY UNA: What!
(LADY UNA stops playing and the music stops).

EMMA: The record isn't playing. The gramophone won't work
without electricity.

LADY UNA: But the music. I heard it…

EMMA: That was you. And it was beautiful.. you said so yourself.

LADY UNA: Me! Then I can play.. I can play. At last! Glory
Alleluia!
(She plays exultantly. TONI enters left)

TONI: Harmony! Quick! The house is on fire.

EMMA: I know. Hush!

TONI: But you can't stay here. I've been searching everywhere for
you.

EMMA: For me? Why?

TONI: Why? Because I was afraid. I thought you might be trapped..

EMMA: And you came to save me. Oh Toni!

TONI: Come away at once. Before it's too late.

EMMA: I'll come with you Toni.. but there's Lady Una.

TONI: *(Calling)* Lady Una!

EMMA: Lady Una! The house is on fire.
(LADY UNA plays on, oblivious to all but her music)

TONI: Can't she hear us? Lady Una!

EMMA: She doesn't want to hear us.

TONI: Madam! *(He makes to go to her but EMMA restrains him)*

EMMA: No, Toni.

TONI: We can't leave her to die.

EMMA: Perhaps she doesn't want to live... now. She has achieved.

TONI: What do you mean?

EMMA: I don't know, but look at her. Have you ever seen her look so happy?

TONI: No...never.

(A crash and burning debris falls outside the window)

TONI: We can't wait any longer.

(He pulls her to the door)

EMMA: I'm coming Toni.

(At the door she turns and looks at LADY UNA).

Goodbye.

(They clasp hands and walk together through the door. A beam splinters and falls outside and the flames leap at the window. LADY UNA plays exultantly as

THE CURTAIN FALLS

PROPERTIES

ACT 1   SCENE 1

ON STAGE

Throne – like chair on dais upstage centre.

'Cello and bow for Lady Una.

Small desk with desk-speaker on dais left of Throne.

Gramophone and record below window up-left, small stool right of
gramophone

Wall mirror right of Throne.

Edwardian armchair on hearthrug before fireplace right

Very modern armchair on hearthrug before fireplace left

Small sideboard right below window

In sideboard drawers table cloth, cutlery, crockery, condiments

Crystal Ball in Lady Una's decoletage

Telescope on mantelpiece left

Wall lights over fireplaces. Hanging chandelier.

OFF STAGE

Ruck-sack containing tweed skirt and lipstick for Emma.

Extending tape-measure in Jefferson's pocket.

Pile of papers, note-book and pencil, large ear-trumpet for Miss
Cowperthwaite

Tin trumpet for Boris.

Steel helmet, gas mask case, pigeon for Rankin.

Collapsible table for Toni.

ACT 2

ON STAGE

Binoculars on mantelpiece right.

OFF STAGE

Dumb waiter on which are all kinds of food for Toni.

Poster ('another Victory!') for Boris.

Cream Puff for Jefferson.

Seven sandwiches for Toni.

ACT 3   SCENE 1

OFF STAGE

Newspaper for Jefferson

Balloon for Boris

Folding screen for Boris

PROPERTIES

ACT 3　　SCENE 2

ON STAGE
Decorations (Festoons etc)
4 free standing candelabra
Dumb waiter, on it crockery, cutlery, wine glasses
Flowers, sausages, etc.
A long table with cloth
5 dining chairs.

OFF STAGE
Bottle of wine for Rankin.
Diamond necklace for Jefferson.

LIGHTING PLOT

ACT 1
Open in full daylight. No cues.
ACT 2
Open in full daylight. No cues.
ACT 3 Scene 1
Full daylight. No cues.
ACT 3 Scene 2
Night. Moonlight through windows. Wall lights and chandeliers on.
Cue 1: "What Happens now?" Blackout except for fires and moonlight.
Cue 2: "Conspiring against my arrangements" Light Candelabra
Cue 3: As Emma appears, spot on Emma.
Cue 4: "Lord have mercy on us". Light begins to turn red. Flame colour shows through windows. Many flashes as rockets explode Continue to curtain.

SOUND PLOT

ACT 1
Cue 1: Opening "La Cygne" on 'Cello.
Cue 2: Switch off gramophone. Cut "La Cygne".
ACT 2
No cues.
ACT 3 Scene 1
No cues.
ACT 3 Scene 2
Cue 1: Gong as Emma appears.
Cue 2: "Thank you Uncle Jeffy". First explosion. From now until final curtain, explosions continue and smoke begins to drift across the room.
Cue 3: "It doesn't work" Start the music of "La Cygne".
Cue 4: "What!" music stops.
Cue 5: "Glory Alleluia!" Lady Una resumes "La Cygne" until curtain.